OUR NATIONAL PARKS
NEED YOU

Our National Parks Need You

Be a Good Human Co
Books for thoughtful and socially-conscious kids.
BeAGoodHuman.Co

Printed in the United States of America.

ISBN 978-1-7366934-4-5 (Hardback)

ISBN 978-1-7366934-3-8 (Paperback)

ISBN 978-1-7366934-5-2 (Ebook)

Library of Congress Control Number: 2022930382

FOR JACK, MY NATIONAL PARK TRAVEL BUDDY. -ST

FOR MY 3 FAVORITE ADVENTURERS, CHRIS, AUGUST, + JUDE, WHO ALWAYS TREAT THE WORLD WITH KINDNESS AND RESPECT. -SA

DEAR KIDS, ADULTS EVERYONE,

WE ARE THE STUDENTS OF CLASSROOM 113.

THE NATIONAL PARKS NEED YOU

FROM THE REDWOOD FOREST,

WE CAN PACK IT OUT WHEN WE LEAVE.

INSTEAD OF GOING UP TO ANIMALS TO GET A CLOSER LOOK,

WE CAN WATCH FROM A DISTANCE SO THEY FEEL SAFE.

INSTEAD OF LEAVING YOUR CAMPFIRE BURNING ALL NIGHT, YOU CAN MAKE SURE IT'S OUT, AND ENJOY A NIGHT

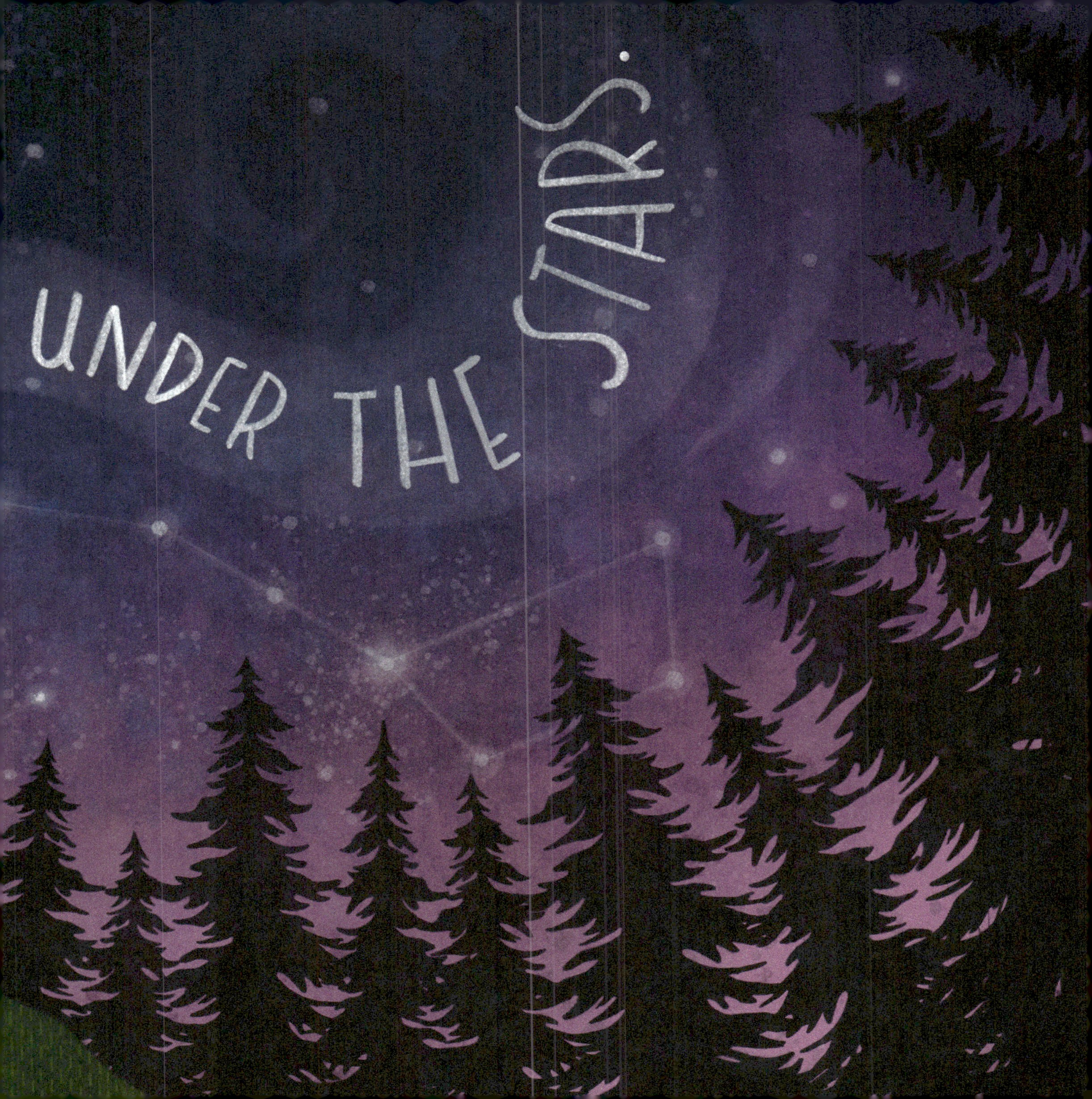
UNDER THE STARS.

INSTEAD OF TAKING SOUVENIRS OUT OF THE PARKS,

WE CAN TAKE PICTURES TO LAST A LIFETIME.

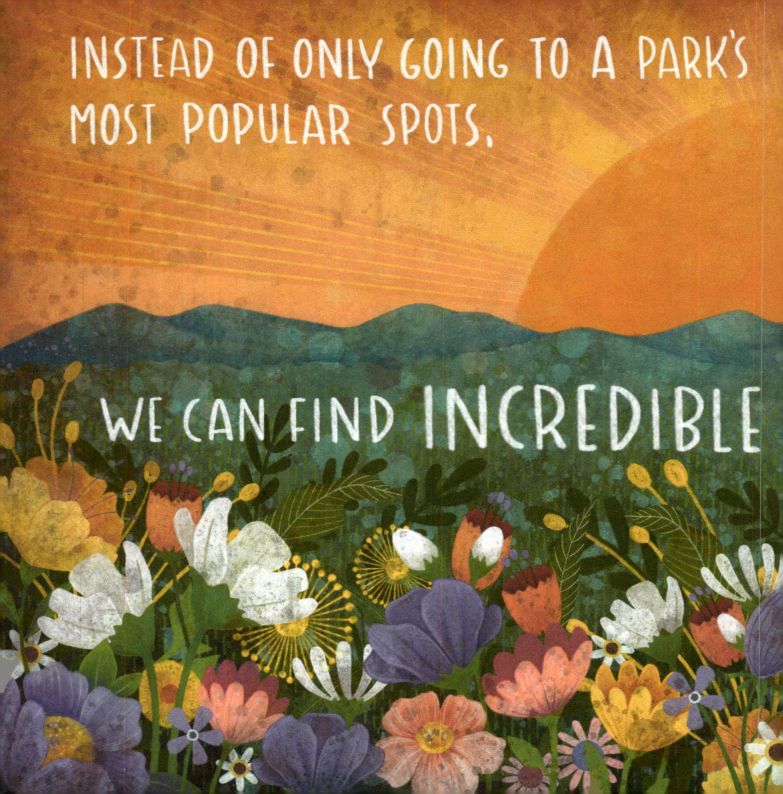

AND DO SO MUCH GOOD FOR NATURE.

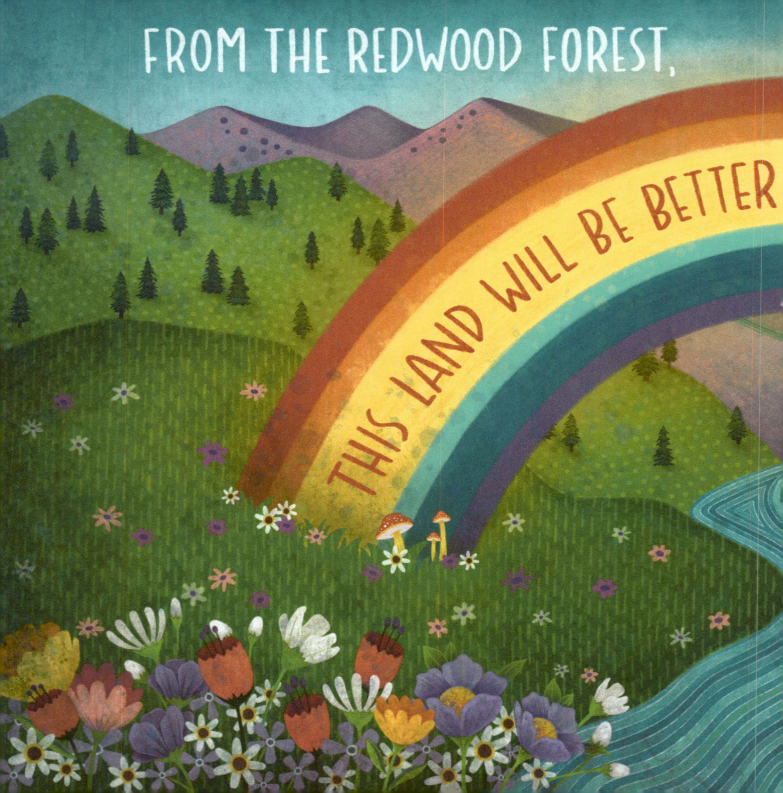

FROM THE REDWOOD FOREST,

THIS LAND WILL BE BETTER

HOW I'M GOING TO HELP

ABOUT THE BOOK

We created this book for all those who love the national parks.

Our National Parks Need You will show kids exactly what they can do to make a difference at parks and public lands around the world. This book doesn't just talk about how we need to be doing more—it actually gives real, actionable ideas. *Our National Parks Need You* is a follow-up to the book, *This Class Can Save the Planet*, which gives kids hands-on ideas on what they can do to help the environment.

Be a Good Human is a publisher on a mission to empower kids, families, and teachers. All books include free educational resources for teachers and schools.

Get our FREE Classroom Kit for this book, which includes worksheets, a poster, and a coloring page!

BeAGoodHuman.co/National-Parks-Classroom-Kit

Stacy Tornio is the author of more than 20 books and the recipient of multiple National Outdoor Book Awards. She's also the creator of Be a Good Human. She lives in Milwaukee, Wisconsin, and is working her way through visiting all of our national parks.

Shannon Andrus is an illustrator, designer and art teacher. Her work can be found all over the country in books, museums, and in various ad campaigns. She lives in Rockford, Michigan, and when not creating, can always be found exploring nature. To see more of Shannon's work, or to purchase the art seen in this book, visit shannonandrusart.com.